Children of the World

Costa Rica

For a free color catalog describing Gareth Stevens' list of high-quality children's books, call
1-800-341-3569 (USA) or 1-800-461-9120 (Canada).

For their help in the preparation of *Children of the World: Costa Rica*, the writer and editors gratefully thank the Friends (Quaker) Peace Center in San José, Costa Rica; Professor Michael Fleet, Marquette University, Milwaukee; Professor Howard Handelman, University of Wisconsin-Milwaukee; and Professor Cecilia Rodriguez, University of Wisconsin-Waukesha.

Flag illustration on page 48, © Flag Research Center.

Library of Congress Cataloging-in-Publication Data

Cummins, Ronnie.
      Costa Rica / written by Ronald Cummins ; photography by Rose Welch.
         p. cm. — (Children of the world)
      Summary: Presents the life of an eleven-year-old girl and her family in Costa Rica, describing her home and school activities and discussing the history, geography, ethnic composition, natural resources, languages, government, religions, culture, and economics of her country.
      ISBN 0-8368-0222-5
      1. Costa Rica—Social life and customs—Juvenile literature. 2. Children—Costa Rica—Juvenile literature. [1. Family life—Costa Rica. 2. Costa Rica.] I. Welch, Rose, ill. II. Title. III. Series: Children of the world (Milwaukee, Wis.)
F1543.8.C86   1990
972.86—dc20   89-43138

A Gareth Stevens Children's Books edition

Edited, designed, and produced by
Gareth Stevens Children's Books
RiverCenter Building, Suite 201
1555 North RiverCenter Drive
Milwaukee, Wisconsin 53212, USA

Series editor: Valerie Weber
Editor: Amy Bauman
Research editor: Kathleen Weisfeld Barrilleaux
Layout: Kate Kriege
Map design: Sheri Gibbs

Printed in the United States of America

1 2 3 4 5 6 7 8 9 96 95 94 93 92 91 90

Children of the World

Costa Rica

Text by Ronnie Cummins
Photography by Rose Welch

Gareth Stevens Children's Books
MILWAUKEE

. . . a note about *Children of the World*:

The children of the world live in fishing towns, Arctic regions, and urban centers, on islands and in mountain valleys, on sheep ranches and fruit farms. This series follows one child in each country through the pattern of his or her life. Candid photographs show the children with their families, at school, at play, and in their communities. The text describes the dreams of the children and, often through their own words, tells how they see themselves and their lives.

Each book also explores events that are unique to the country in which the child lives, including festivals, religious ceremonies, and national holidays. The *Children of the World* series does more than tell about foreign countries. It introduces the children of each country and shows readers what it is like to be a child in that country.

Children of the World includes the following published and soon-to-be-published titles:

Australia	El Salvador	Japan	Spain
Bhutan	England	Jordan	Sweden
Bolivia	Finland	Malaysia	Tanzania
Brazil	France	Mexico	Thailand
Burkina Faso	Greece	Nepal	Turkey
Burma	Guatemala	New Zealand	USSR
China	Hong Kong	Nicaragua	Vietnam
Costa Rica	Hungary	Philippines	West Germany
Cuba	India	Singapore	Yugoslavia
Czechoslovakia	Indonesia	South Africa	Zambia
Egypt	Italy	South Korea	

. . . and about *Costa Rica*:

Eleven-year-old Cristiana lives in a mountain village, where she works on her family's small dairy farm and in their modest restaurant. She plans to study agriculture in college. Meanwhile, she's happy to ride her horse along mountain trails.

To enhance this book's value in libraries and classrooms, comprehensive reference sections include up-to-date information about Costa Rica's geography, demographics, language, currency, education, culture, industry, and natural resources. *Costa Rica* also features a bibliography, research topics, activity projects, and discussions of such subjects as San José, the country's history, political system, and ethnic and religious composition.

The living conditions and experiences of children in Costa Rica may vary, but all enjoy a high standard of living and broad educational opportunities. The reference sections help bring to life for young readers the uniqueness of Costa Rica's development. Of particular interest are discussions of Costa Rica's disbandment of its army, its unusually stable government, and its commitment to peace among its Central American neighbors.

CONTENTS

LIVING IN COSTA RICA:
Cristiana, a Farm Girl from the Mountains

Eleven-year-old Evelyn Cristiana Gonzáles-Hidalgo lives on a farm in the mountain village of Sacramento, Costa Rica. Cristiana and her family live in a wooden house overlooking the slopes of Barva, one of Costa Rica's tallest volcanoes. Cristiana's family includes her parents, Obdulio and Ana Beliza; her brother, Uriel; and her sister, Olga Patricia. Olga, who is 15, attends high school in Heredia, a town in the valley below Sacramento.

The small village of Sacramento usually doesn't show on maps of Costa Rica. Cristiana says she is glad to live in this friendly community. All of the several hundred residents know one another and many are related. Cristiana is surrounded by her grandparents and many uncles, aunts, and cousins. Their houses and farms are scattered all throughout the area.

Opposite: In a rare quiet moment, the Gonzáles-Hidalgo family gathers outside their mountain home in Sacramento. With Cristiana are her parents, Obdulio and Ana Beliza, and her brother, Uriel. Olga, Cristiana's older sister, is away at school. ▶

The family never tires of the view from their Sacramento home. At 7,000 feet (2,100 m) above sea level, Sacramento lies above both Heredia and San José on the slopes of Barva Volcano. At this height, much of the mountain stretches out below the small farming village.

Obdulio works as a carpenter for a hotel near Sacramento when he's not working on the family farm or in the restaurant.

Cristiana's Home and Family Farm

Cristiana and her family live on a small dairy farm. In addition to caring for the cows, chickens, and horses, they also tend a garden in which they grow most of their own vegetables and fruits. And if that isn't enough to keep everyone busy, the family also runs a restaurant, which is attached to the house. There, Cristiana's parents serve delicious homemade dishes to both tourists and local people.

Cristiana's father, Obdulio, is a skilled carpenter. He built the family's five-room house with the help of relatives and friends. Traditionally, relatives, friends, and neighbors pitch in whenever a family builds a house or barn. They cut the lumber from neighboring forests and do the work by hand without the use of electrical tools.

Ana Beliza manages the family restaurant, although everyone helps out.

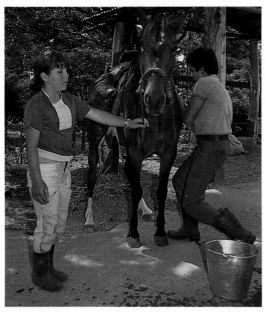

Now that he is 14, Uriel handles many of the farm tasks.

Cristiana helps out at home, on the farm, in the restaurant, or wherever she can.

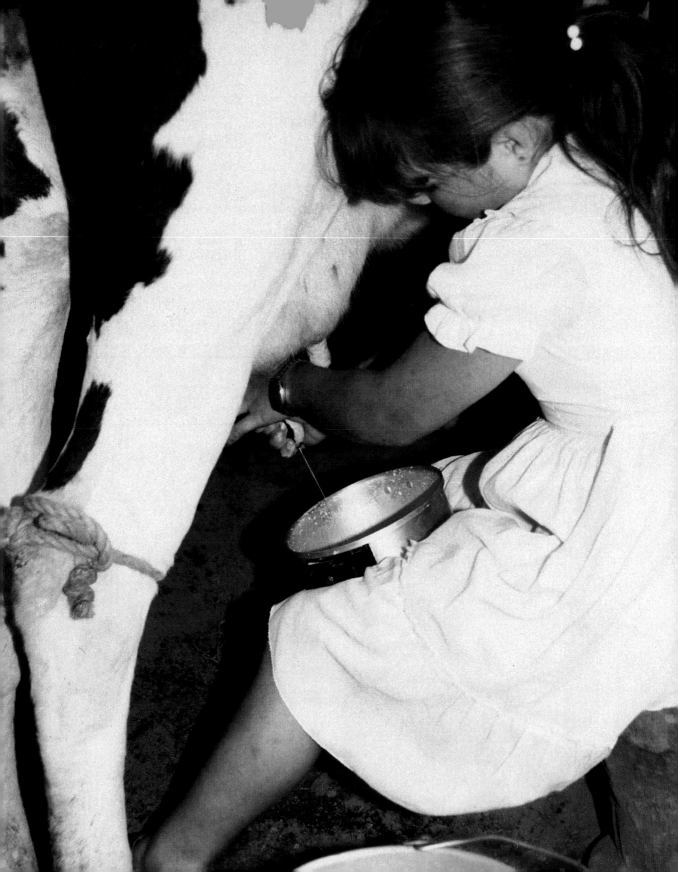

A Typical Morning for the Sacramento Farm Girl

Cristiana's day begins at 5:30 a.m. She wakes, dresses, and hurries to the pasture to bring the cows in for milking. Although it's barely light outside, this is one of Cristiana's favorite times of day. The birds sing from trees against the colorful sunrise sky, and the air feels fresh and cool. Peacefulness fills Cristiana as she tends to the four dairy cows. In the barn, after securing the cows in their harnesses, she feeds and washes them. Finally, sitting on a low wooden stool, she milks each cow by hand.

After milking them, Cristiana leads the cows back out to the pasture. Walking back to the house, she remembers learning to milk the cows when she was just seven years old. She can now milk a cow as well as most adults. Smiling to herself, she carries the stainless steel pail full of fresh milk into the house.

◀ Opposite: It takes strong hands to milk the cows.

Left: Carrying a pail of fresh milk, Cristiana heads back toward the house where she knows that breakfast will be waiting.
Below: Before leaving for school, Cristiana leads the cows back to the pasture where they graze all day.

Fresh tomatoes from the garden add color to Cristiana's waiting breakfast.

By 6:30, Cristiana sits down to breakfast, which usually consists of rice, black beans, fried *plátanos* (a type of banana), and *café con leche* (coffee with milk). A hot breakfast tastes good after she has been working outside in the chilly morning air.

After breakfast, Cristiana finishes her chores. School doesn't begin until 11:00 a.m., so she has plenty of time. She begins by splitting wood, which is one of her favorite chores. Although she is small, Cristiana is quite strong, so she swings her axe with no trouble. Sometimes Uriel helps her, and they have a contest to see who can split the most wood in five minutes. As usual, Cristiana splits enough wood to last the whole day. Like everyone else in the village, the family cooks and heats with a wood stove. Even though it never snows in Sacramento, it gets quite cool at night and in the early mornings. Without the stove's heat on those frosty mornings, Cristiana knows she'd never get out of bed.

Left and opposite: Cristiana pulls wood from a woodpile for splitting. Then, using an axe that is almost taller than she is, she splits the wood into pieces small enough to fit into the stove. ▶

After splitting firewood, Cristiana feeds the chickens and the geese, calling them with a clucking sound as she throws out kernels of corn.   Finally, Cristiana feeds her favorite animal — her puppy, Caballito. Caballito, whose name is Spanish for "little horse," gets a bowl of milk and some stale bread. By the time Cristiana has finished feeding the animals, it's nine o'clock.

Cristiana thinks feeding the turkeys, geese, and chickens is more fun than work. But just in case an especially hungry bird should mistake her toes for kernels of corn, Cristiana keeps her distance.

Preparing for school, Cristiana shines her shoes and puts on her uniform — a blue skirt and a white shirt — similar to that worn by most Costa Rican schoolgirls. Cristiana doesn't mind wearing a uniform; she is used to it. School rules require the students to wear uniforms, and Cristiana can't imagine dressing any other way. In addition, her parents say that if schools didn't require uniforms, many families would not be able to afford school clothes for their children.

Since Caballito eats so quickly, Cristiana always has time to play with him before school.

Cristiana works at putting a shine on her school shoes.

Having her hair brushed out is one of the most relaxing chores of the morning.

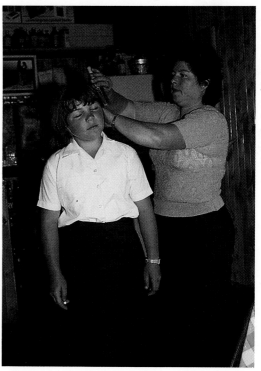

Cristiana's Elementary School

Cristiana has only a short walk from her house to the school, but it's a steep climb up the mountain road. Green pastures and a soccer field surround the two-room schoolhouse, Escuela Lourdes, which has only 30 students and one teacher. Over the years, the small school has earned a reputation for its excellent teachers.

Cristiana and the other children go to school for nine months a year and have a long vacation in November and December. In her elementary school, grades one through three attend classes in the morning, while grades four through six attend classes from 11:00 a.m. until 3:00 p.m. Cristiana's fourth- and fifth-grade class has three boys and eight girls, including her friend, Liliana, who is also 11 years old. Together the girls study history, reading, writing, geography, math, science, and art. Cristiana hopes someday to attend college, where she'd like to study agriculture.

◀ Opposite: Cristiana knows all the shortcuts to school through neighboring pastures and across streambeds.
Below: Cristiana, Liliana (farthest right), and their classmates pose with their teacher, Melvin Chavéz, outside of the schoolhouse, Escuela Lourdes.

For junior and senior high school, Sacramento students must travel to Heredia. This means a 30-minute walk to the bus stop each morning and then an hour's ride on the bus. People in Sacramento don't travel much and think this is a long trip. To avoid it, some students, like Olga, live with relatives in Heredia and return home only on weekends. If Olga goes on to college, she will go to school either in Heredia or in San José, which is even farther.

Today, Cristiana's teacher, *Don* Melvin, gives a lesson about the rain forest. (In Spanish, use of the title *Don* or *Doña* before a first name is a sign of respect.) He tells the students how important it is for Costa Rica and other countries to preserve their remaining rain forests, because they help protect a vital layer of Earth's atmosphere, called the ozone layer. The ozone shields Earth from the sun's harmful ultraviolet rays. As part of their studies, Don Melvin has scheduled a class trip to a nearby rain forest. The forest fascinates Cristiana, so she looks forward to the class trip.

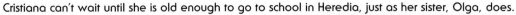

Cristiana can't wait until she is old enough to go to school in Heredia, just as her sister, Olga, does.

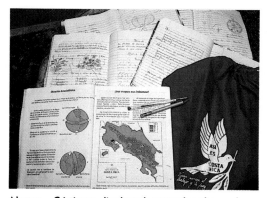

Above: Cristiana displays her textbooks and notebooks against her book bag.
Right: During a geography lesson, some of Cristiana's classmates refer to the globe to locate the areas where rain forests grow.

Cristiana and her classmates crowd around Don Melvin as he gives a lecture on Costa Rica's dwindling rain forests.

At recess, the students play their favorite games of *policía y ladrónes* (cops and robbers), and hide-and-seek. Then, just before classes start again, the children eat a snack prepared by Doña Teresita, who owns the restaurant across the street from the school. Usually the snack consists of a fresh fruit drink and a corn tortilla filled with cheese and sausage.

Left: The many bushes and trees surrounding the school offer ample hiding places for a good game of hide-and-seek.
Below: Recess allows Cristiana and her classmates the chance to vent their energies.

Compared to other Latin American countries, Costa Rica spends a large percentage of its budget on education. The government can afford this, in part, because the constitution of 1948 abolished the country's army. Headed by José Figueres Ferrer, the government saw this as a way to bring peace to Costa Rica. Today, Costa Rica spends very little on weapons or defense. The money this saves goes toward education and other social services. When Cristiana reads about wars being fought all over the world, she is proud that her country abolished its army.

Above: After particularly rough play at recess, Cristiana and her friend Liliana wash up before going back to class.
Below: Before class starts again, the children devour their midday snack.

Below: Although Doña Teresita prepares the snack, the children clean up afterward.

Cristiana Visits the Farm

Cristiana often visits her grandparents on their farm. One of her favorite things about the farm is the large, colorful flower garden that her great-grandmother planted years ago. Cristiana and her grandmother often stroll among the flowers, looking for new blooms. Cristiana cuts some to take home. Winding through the garden, Cristiana imagines her great-grandmother walking the same paths.

Cristiana and her grandmother spend a lot of time walking and talking in the garden that surrounds the house.

Cristiana cuts fresh flowers to decorate the restaurant.

On weekends, Cristiana helps her grandparents milk their cows. They milk the 20 cows by hand, so it's quite a difficult task. During the week, Cristiana's father and her Uncle Martin help her grandfather do the milking. They then run the milk through an electrically powered cooler, which helps prevent the growth of harmful bacteria. Later, they strain the milk and pour it into sterilized steel containers. Cristiana's grandmother saves some of the milk to make cheese and sour cream.

Below: Uncle Martin patiently strains the cooled milk through the cheesecloth.

Cristiana leads Pajarito down the road to meet the milkman.

The milkman exchanges empty milk containers for the full ones Cristiana brings him.

As part of her chores, Cristiana delivers the fresh milk to the milkman. She doesn't mind this task, because it means spending time with the family's horse, Pajarito. With the help of her brother, Cristiana straps the milk containers onto Pajarito's back and leads him about a half mile (1 km) down the road. There, she waits for the milkman, who loads the containers into his truck and takes them down into the valley, where he delivers the milk door to door.

A plate of her grandmother's pastries tempts Cristiana.

Uncle Martin joins Cristiana for something to eat. After a morning of hard work, everything tastes especially good.

By the time Cristiana returns to the house, it's time for a break. Everyone piles into the kitchen, where her grandmother has prepared a meal of bread, fresh cheese, and homemade pastries. Coffee brews on the stove, too. As Cristiana breathes in its rich scent, she understands why Costa Rica is famous for its coffee. When she has eaten her fill, Cristiana turns on the radio. Leaning back, she takes a moment to relax and listen to the music. Many of her favorite songs are in English and were recorded in the United States. She wonders if the songs are still popular there.

Cristiana tunes in a station, hoping to find some of her favorite songs.

A colorful sign calls passing travelers into La Campesina.

Ana Beliza attends to food cooking on the huge stove that serves the restaurant.

La Campesina, the Gonzáles-Hidalgo Family Restaurant

Obdulio built the family restaurant a year ago. Called *La Campesina*, Spanish for "the country woman," it is popular with both local people and tourists. Over the wood stove in the kitchen, Cristiana's parents prepare the food — much of which is produced on the Gonzáles farm. Specialties include hearty soups, shish kebabs, *flan de coco* (coconut custard), and fresh sour cream and tortillas.

The family works together to run the restaurant and to keep up with the milking, the garden, and the other chores. Cristiana often helps out in the kitchen and has learned many of her mother's cooking skills. At times when she's working, Cristiana wishes she could be outside riding her horse or playing with her friends. Her mother understands this and sometimes tells Cristiana to go and play even before the work is finished.

During the week, the Gonzáles family serves only a few customers. But on Saturdays and Sundays, people suddenly crowd the restaurant. When that happens, Cristiana's mother, father, and aunt all work in the kitchen.

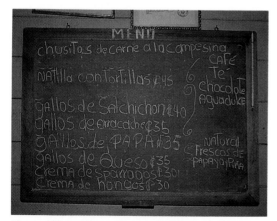

Above: The restaurant menu hangs where everyone can see it. Part of Cristiana's job is to keep the menu updated. Because Obdulio often makes fresh desserts, the menu items change almost daily.
Right: While everyone else is busy in the kitchen, Cristiana keeps the dining area clean.

Many of the restaurant customers are people passing through Sacramento on weekend visits to Braulio Carrillo National Park. This park — one of Costa Rica's many national parks — is located just 2.5 miles (4 km) up the road. But Cristiana thinks that many people come just for the view of Costa Rica's Central Valley from the back of their restaurant. At night, thousands of lights twinkle in San José below them. Although Cristiana and her family have lived on the mountain all their lives, they never tire of its beauty.

Below: The colorful lights of San José flood the valley below Sacramento. Cristiana and her family also take pleasure in the view and know that many of their customers do, too.

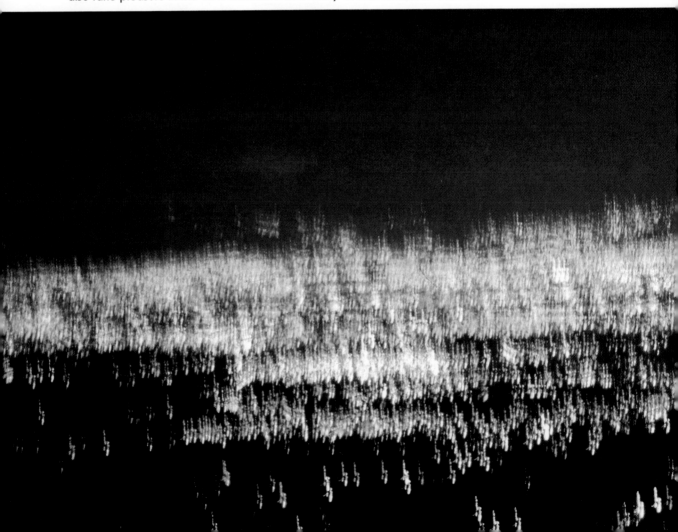

Cristiana's father is building an outdoor patio so that their customers can sit outside and enjoy the magnificent view. As he measures and cuts the lumber or pounds nails, he explains each step to Cristiana and Uriel. Cristiana listens to his every word, and she notices that Uriel listens just as eagerly. Working with her father makes Cristiana feel close to him.

Right: During a slow time at the restaurant, Obdulio turns his attention to the outdoor patio.

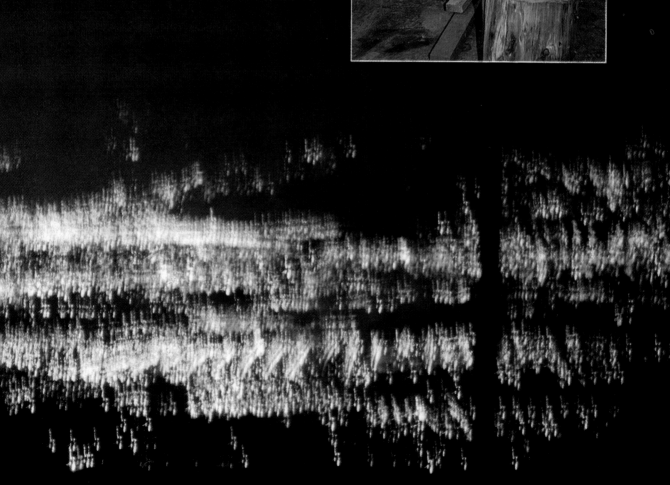

Free Time for Cristiana

When she has a little free time, Cristiana usually goes looking for her friends Liliana and Maria. Some days, the girls walk to Cristiana's family farm. If they don't have much time, they walk only as far as the store near their school. The store, which is owned by Doña Teresita, serves as a local gathering place. The children can usually find something to do there.

Uriel saddles Pajarito for Cristiana.

◀ Opposite: It won't be long until Cristiana's feet reach the stirrups.
Below: Cristiana's trip to the potato patch proves worth the ride.

Cristiana spends some afternoons riding Pajarito. After Uriel finishes milking cows at his grandparents' farm, he brings the horse back with him to the house. With his help, Cristiana then saddles Pajarito for a ride. Today, Cristiana's mother has asked her to ride out to the potato patch on her grandparents' farm to see if any of the potatoes are ready to harvest. Cristiana gallops away down the road, wishing that she didn't have school or chores to worry about so she could ride Pajarito all day.

Cristiana spends some of her afternoons alone reading, watching television, and doing her homework. On these days, she waits for her father to finish his work and then asks him to take her for a ride on his motorcycle. Cristiana thinks there's nothing like riding up and down the mountain roads on a motorcycle. As the wind rushes at them, she holds tightly to her father.

Obdulio revs the motorcycle's engine as he and Cristiana get ready for a spin up the mountain. The turns make Cristiana's heart pound.

Not all of Cristiana's afternoons are as hair-raising. Here she curls up with the many dolls and toys that share her bed.

When Olga is away from home, Cristiana has their bedroom all to herself. Although she misses her sister very much, having her own room makes Cristiana feel grown-up.

Today, without being asked, Cristiana straightens her bedroom. She carefully arranges her dolls and stuffed animals on her bed. They keep her company until Olga comes home from Heredia on the weekends. All week long, Cristiana looks forward to seeing Olga and hearing stories about what's been happening in Heredia. With a population of 30,000, that city is quite different from Sacramento. Heredia entices Cristiana with its shops, movie theaters, and large public swimming pool. In three years, she will attend the junior high school there, and she can hardly wait.

A typical breakfast consists of corn tortillas, a bowl of fresh sour cream, and café con leche.

Her mother's shish kebabs make Cristiana hungry any time of day.

Obdulio's flan de coco has given the restaurant a reputation for having mouth-watering desserts.

Heredia's tropical fruit stands attract many buyers. Many of the fruits offered, such as bananas and pineapples, are grown farther down the slopes of Barva.

The Market and Typical Foods of Heredia

Because the small village store can't carry everything that the people need, the family travels to Heredia's market for certain items. The city is a long bus ride away, but Cristiana gladly seizes the chance to go. Once there, she and Uriel ignore the vendors selling potatoes, carrots, squash, and beans; these they can find in Sacramento. Instead, they browse among the tropical fruits, such as bananas and pineapples, which are grown on the lower slopes of the mountains and along the coasts.

Traditional Costa Rican foods include tortillas, rice, beans, potatoes, eggs, and fruit. The family chooses their breakfast and lunch from these. In the evening, Ana Beliza serves a meat or cheese dish with a fresh salad. Sometimes, a fresh dessert tops off the meal. When Obdulio makes desserts for the restaurant, he makes extra for the family. Tonight they're eating flan de coco.

Sunday Church Services in Sacramento

Cristiana looks forward to Sundays, when life seems to run a little slower than it does the rest of the week. Sundays in Sacramento are quiet, and most activity centers on church services. Like many other Costa Ricans, Cristiana and her family belong to the Roman Catholic church. Sacramento's small Catholic church perches on the mountainside not far from the Gonzáles-Hidalgo home. Everyone in Cristiana's family attends, as do many of their friends and neighbors.

Before Mass, Cristiana arranges flowers from her grandmother's garden around the church altar.

The congregation listens intently as the village priest begins the Mass.

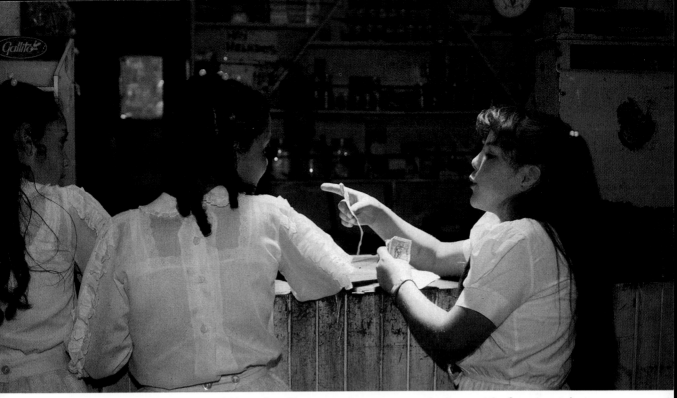

Between catechism class and Mass, the village store becomes a gathering spot for Sacramento's young people. Cristiana and her friends often walk there to buy a snack or to visit with other friends.

On Sunday mornings, Cristiana attends catechism, or religious instruction, class. The class lasts for two hours, after which she and her friends can play until church services start at 1:00 p.m. Sometimes, they run to Doña Teresita's store up the road to buy cookies and cold drinks. Today, they stand outside the store talking excitedly about tomorrow's school trip to the national park.

Doña Teresita packs the store shelves with groceries to keep up with her customers' needs.

A Class Field Trip to the National Park

A truck full of eager explorers rattles its way up the mountainside to the national park.

Once out of the truck, Cristiana and the other children scramble along the trail toward the volcano crater.

As part of their ecology studies, Cristiana's class has planned a trip to Braulio Carrillo National Park. This park, located atop the same mountain on which Sacramento sits, includes about 80,000 acres (32,000 ha) of rain forest. Cristiana is eager to explore the rain forest, where the trees grow so thick that they block the sky. She knows that many wild animals and over 850 different kinds of birds live in the forest. From her father, she has learned to identify many of them.

The class climbs into the back of a pickup truck for the short trip to the park. The truck winds up the mountain road, moving slowly because of the steep incline. When the truck reaches the park entrance, the explorers quickly pile out. They begin their tour by hiking about 1.2 miles (2 km) to the old crater of Barva Volcano. This volcano last erupted over a thousand years ago, and a lake with cold, clear water now fills its crater.

People can drink the cold, pure water that now fills the old crater of Barva Volcano.

Having completed the trek to the crater, Cristiana and her class pose victoriously before its sign.

Don Melvin gives the students a lesson on using a compass. He reminds them that a group of tourists lost its way in the dense forest near here several weeks before. The tourists wandered for two weeks before finding the trail again. Because they had studied the forest, they knew which wild plants, nuts, and berries to eat. Cristiana remembers seeing that story on television and thinks it would be frightening to be lost. She and Liliana stick close together.

After eating lunch on top of the volcano, the children play hide-and-seek, being careful not to go too far into the woods. When they tire of the game, they hike along a forest trail, stopping now and then to study the plant life. They finally turn onto the main trail and start back to the truck. After hiking in the dense forest, the trail seems very sunny. By the time they reach the truck, everyone is tired, and although the ride back to the school is bumpy, no one notices.

Above: The students listen carefully as Don Melvin explains how to use a compass. No one thinks getting lost sounds like much fun.
Left: Cristiana and a friend examine a huge fern growing along the path.

Above: The class lunches on top of the volcano. Cristiana and a friend find a sturdy log to sit on.
Left: Tortillas filled with sausage, egg, and cheese. Banana leaves make handy sandwich wraps.

Below: Juicy melon slices hit the spot.
Right: After a full lunch, everyone is ready for a game of hide-and-seek.

43

Planting Trees: A Lesson in Forest Preservation

After visiting Braulio Carrillo National Park, Cristiana's class researches the rain forest. They learn that in 1950, 72% of Costa Rica was covered by forests. Today, the forests cover only 25% of the country. The class decides to do something to help preserve the forest. As a class project, they plant trees in the schoolyard. Each student is responsible for one tree.

Cristiana and her classmates plant four kinds of trees that are native to the area: *chile, quisarra, coquito,* and *cacho venado.* Then, the class mails a letter to the Costa Rican government, asking that more land be set aside to protect the rain forest. Cristiana imagines what her tree will look like when it is grown. She hopes that by the time she is an adult, all people will value Earth as much as she values her little tree.

Opposite: Cristiana and a friend carry water from the school to feed the new trees. The students know they will have to make this trip daily until the rainy season begins. ▶

Above: Cristiana lowers her tree into a hole and covers it with soil.
Below: The students fence in the trees with small sticks. Hopefully, this will protect them from chickens that roam the schoolyard.

The forest rises above the mist of the valley.

From the yard of her home, Cristiana
waves good-bye.

FOR YOUR INFORMATION: Costa Rica

Official Name: Republica de Costa Rica
(ray-POOH-blee-kah day KOHS-tah REE-kah)
Republic of Costa Rica

Capital: San José (SAHN hoe-SAY)

History

The Native Inhabitants of Costa Rica

Before Christopher Columbus and the Spanish explorers sailed to the New
World, native tribes of Indians had lived in the Costa Rica region for thousands
of years. When the Spaniards arrived, the Costa Rican area was dominated by
two major Indian nations: the Chorotega and the Chibcha.

Mountains rise beyond a sweep of modern-looking buildings in the capital city of San José.

Ancestors of the Chorotega originally lived in ancient Mexico but fled their homelands when enemies tried to enslave them. In their native language, *Chorotega* means "people who are fleeing." The Chorotega then settled in the northwest portion of present-day Costa Rica, near the Pacific Ocean. There they built cities in which as many as 20,000 people lived.

The Chorotega lived as hunters, fishermen, and farmers. They were especially skilled farmers, and grew corn, cotton, beans, squash, fruit, and cacao. They also established themselves as fine artisans, creating beautiful weavings, pottery works, and jade carvings. Over time, the Chorotega developed a complex society. Tribal lands, for example, became the shared property of everyone, and the harvests were divided among the families according to need. They also developed a calendar, recorded their stories on parchment, and established a monetary system that used cacao seeds as currency.

The Chibcha Indians, another major native group, migrated to Costa Rica from Colombia. The Chibcha, who lived in fortified towns, are remembered for the

beautiful gold and stone objects that they created. Many of these objects were large spheres carved out of solid granite that can be seen in Costa Rica even today. The Chibcha carefully arranged these spheres near their cemeteries and on an island called the Isle of Palms. Some of the spheres are as small as oranges, while others are huge globes almost 6 feet (2 m) in diameter. Why the Chibcha constructed these perfectly rounded spheres remains a mystery.

One of the mysterious Chibcha spheres is displayed in a courtyard of the National Museum.

The Colonial Era in Costa Rica: 1502-1821

The first European to set foot on what is now Costa Rica was Christopher Columbus. In 1502, Columbus, on his fourth and last voyage to the Americas, was sailing along the eastern coast of Central America when a sudden storm forced him and his crew to seek shelter. The men anchored their ships off the Caribbean coast of Costa Rica, where the port of Limón is now located.

For several weeks, Columbus and his men remained in Costa Rica, resting and repairing their ships after the long voyage from Spain. While exploring, Columbus's crew came upon several of the area's Indian tribes and were awed by their gold jewelry and other ornaments. Based on these encounters, Columbus returned to Spain and reported that the area was rich with gold.

From this claim, the area became known as *Costa Rica*, which is Spanish for "rich coast." Columbus also noted that the area was full of gentle, friendly natives. The Spaniards decided this meant they would be easy to conquer.

The Spanish conquistadores who followed Columbus did not find the Costa Rica that Columbus had described. The area was not rich with gold, and the Indians fought the Spanish invasion — of both soldiers and the missionaries who followed them — with all their strength. Thousands of Indians died, killed either by the Spaniards or by the diseases that they brought over with them from Europe. Rather than be enslaved, many surviving Indians fled Costa Rica.

It was not until 1564 that Don Juan Vásquez de Coronado established the first permanent Spanish settlement in Costa Rica. Through his efforts, the area was finally opened to colonization for the first time. It was also Coronado who introduced domesticated animals such as horses, pigs, and cows to Costa Rica. By the beginning of the 1600s, very few Costa Rican Indians still lived inside the country. The Spaniards began capturing blacks in the Caribbean islands and bringing them back to Costa Rica to work as servants on Spanish plantations.

But Spanish colonies did not flourish. For one thing, Costa Rica was a long and difficult sea voyage or overland trek from the Spanish Empire's colonial centers in Guatemala and Mexico. Eventually, because the colony had just a few slaves and not enough gold, the Spaniards lost interest in the area. For several centuries Costa Rica became one of the "forgotten colonies" of New Spain. By 1800, only about 50,000 people lived in the entire country.

The Rise of an Independent Nation

In the fall of 1821, news arrived in Costa Rica that the other Central American colonies had declared independence from Spain. Costa Rica soon joined its neighbors in their bid for freedom. This ended Spanish domination in the New World. After a brief period of Mexican control, Costa Rica and the other colonies, which included Guatemala, El Salvador, Honduras, Nicaragua, and the modern Mexican state of Chiapas, formed the short-lived Central American Federation (1823-1838). When the union fell apart, Costa Rica declared its own independence and Braulio Carrillo Colina became president.

Although Carrillo ruled as a dictator, suppressing any opposition to his will, he organized the country's political system. He did the same for the country's economy, mainly by encouraging the people to produce coffee as a way to generate money. When Costa Rica's soil and climate conditions proved to be ideal for the coffee plant, the country became the first Central American nation to grow coffee on a large scale. By the mid-1800s, coffee beans had become Costa Rica's leading export, and the country's economy and population began to expand. As the country grew, the government built cities, roads, and schools and introduced public education.

Despite the good Carrillo did for Costa Rica, people resented his dictatorship. In 1842, rebels led by Francisco Morazán forced Carrillo from power. Morazán, who had led the Central American Federation, became the new president and at once tried to reestablish the union. But by this time, the Costa Rican people were used to seeing their nation as separate. They revolted and, in a very short time, removed Morazán from the presidency. Several years and several leaders later, Costa Rica drew up a new constitution declaring itself a republic.

The Invasion of William Walker

In 1855, a US citizen named William Walker invaded Central America with a band of heavily armed followers. Walker dreamed of conquering all of Central America and annexing his empire to the United States as additional slave territory. Walker hoped that the addition of new slave states would strengthen the proslavery movement in the United States. Walker's troops first invaded Nicaragua, where during fierce battles, they captured or killed many Nicaraguans. In 1856, Walker named himself "President of the Republic of Nicaragua" and then sent some of his troops to invade Costa Rica. By this time, Walker's actions had angered many Central Americans. Thousands of volunteers from throughout the region rose up to fight against him. In Costa Rica, President Juan Rafael Mora, who was then in power, declared war on Walker's invading army, and 9,000 volunteers joined the fight.

In April 1856 at the famous Battle of Rivas, the Costa Rican and Central American volunteer forces defeated Walker's army and regained their independence. From this battle, Costa Rica gained a hero in a young drummer boy named Juan Santamaría. When Walker's troops barricaded themselves in a building, Santamaría ran forward and set fire to it. Walker's forces killed Juan Santamaría, and he is now honored as Costa Rica's national hero of independence.

Costa Rica Today

By combining policies of peace and social sharing, Costa Rica has developed and prospered, becoming one of the Western Hemisphere's most peaceful and democratic nations. In fact, Costa Rica is often called the "Switzerland of Latin America." Like Switzerland, Costa Rica avoids conflict or war with its neighbors. Costa Rica, in fact, has abolished its army. Like Switzerland, it also imposes high taxes on its businesses and wealthy people and uses this tax money to fund welfare and social programs. And, like Switzerland, much of Costa Rica is covered with beautiful mountains.

Achieving this state of peaceful democracy has meant struggle. In 1948, for example, President Rafael Angel Calderón Guardia refused to hand over power to the newly elected president, Otilio Ulate Blanco. Civil war broke out with the forces opposing Calderón led by José Figueres Ferrer. Figueres and his forces defeated the army and came to power after a short but bloody uprising. Figueres became chairman of the revolutionary junta, or ruling body.

As the leader, Figueres drafted a new constitution. This constitution abolished the armed forces, prohibited presidents from being elected twice in a row, gave everyone over 18 the right to vote, and established a powerful, neutral body to oversee future elections. The government reformed systems for taxes, health care, social security, and education. It set taxes according to income; wealthy people paid more and poor people paid less. It provided health care, social security, and public education for everyone. It took control of banks, insurance companies, public transportation, energy, housing construction, and telecommunications to ensure that they were run for everyone's best interest.

In 1949, Figueres turned executive power over to Ulate Blanco, the rightfully elected president. Over the next 40 years, Figueres's reforms were continued and extended. Figueres himself was later elected president. The government drafted laws to protect the environment and to provide for the poor. It extended social welfare programs and invested much money in education.

Costa Rica is today considered a model of democracy. The country enjoys one of the highest standards of living in Latin America despite debts that have grown in recent years. To pay these debts, the government has reduced social services and raised the prices of basic consumer goods. Still, its educational, cultural, ecological, and health care programs compare favorably with far richer, larger nations such as the United States or Canada. The wealth of these programs is partially the result of Costa Rica's tax structure established by Figueres's constitution, as well as large amounts of foreign aid coming primarily from the United States. Also, since the country has no army, it spends almost no money on weapons or defense. Its defense budget supports just 8,500 police officers. (Most of these police officers are armed with billy clubs instead of guns.) Costa Rica's leaders say that the country doesn't need an army. They believe that if any country were to invade Costa Rica, the world community would immediately condemn that country for attacking an unarmed state.

In 1987, Costa Rica's president, Oscar Arias Sánchez, organized meetings of regional leaders to promote peace in the war-torn countries of Nicaragua, Guatemala, El Salvador, and Honduras. For his efforts, Arias was awarded the Nobel Peace Prize that year. His term ended in early 1990. At that time, the people elected Rafael Angel Calderón, Jr. their new president. Calderón is the son of former president Rafael Angel Calderón Guardia.

Government

According to the constitution of 1949, Costa Rica is a republic whose government is divided into three branches: executive, legislative, and judicial. The president serves as the head of the executive branch and is assisted by two vice-presidents and a presidentially appointed cabinet. The president, who serves a four-year term, must receive at least 40% of all votes cast and cannot be reelected. The law requires everyone 18 years old or older to vote, and usually 80% or more of the eligible citizens actually vote.

The one-house Legislative Assembly has 57 members, called deputies, elected from the country's seven provinces for four-year terms. In Costa Rica's Legislative Assembly, as in Canada's House of Commons and the US House of Representatives, the number of members from a given province or state depends upon population. In 1986, Dr. Rosemary Karpinski was elected president of the National Assembly, thus becoming the first woman in Central America to head a legislative branch of government.

The Supreme Court of Justice heads the country's judicial branch, which includes over 100 lower courts. The Legislative Assembly elects the court's 17 justices, or magistrates, who serve eight-year terms. At a term's end, the magistrates automatically reassume their duties unless voted out by the Legislative Assembly.

Presidentially appointed governors head Costa Rica's seven provinces. Locally elected governments have limited powers and cannot pass laws that affect national policy. These local governments have begun to demand more power and control over public tax money. After a recent series of strikes and road blockades, former president Arias promised the local governments that they will receive 10% of all federal funds for local needs.

Population and Ethnic Groups

Costa Rica's population of approximately 2,800,000 people consists of several different ethnic groups. People of European (primarily Spanish) descent make up about 87%; mestizos (European-Indian blood), about 7%; blacks, about 3%; Chinese, about 2%; Native Americans and others, about 1%. About three-fourths of the people live in the highlands, with the remainder of the population scattered along the coasts and in the lowlands. Residents of the highlands and of the Central Valley live mostly in rural areas or small towns and are largely of European (mainly Spanish) descent. Many of these people are farmers and coffee growers. Mestizos live along the Pacific coast, and blacks live mainly on the Caribbean coast, where many of their ancestors settled when they were brought to Costa Rica from Jamaica.

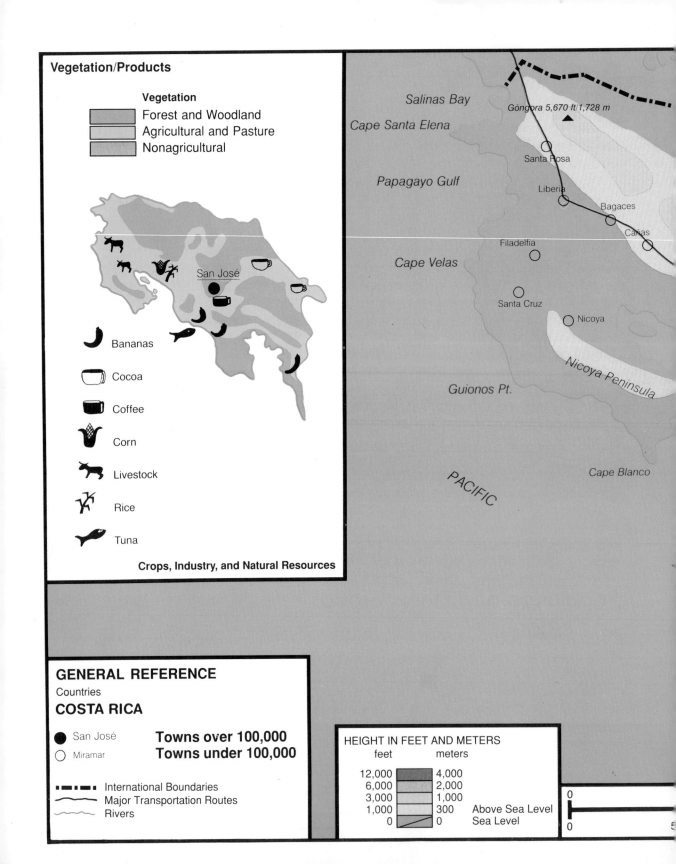

Vegetation/Products

Vegetation

Forest and Woodland
Agricultural and Pasture
Nonagricultural

San José

Bananas

Cocoa

Coffee

Corn

Livestock

Rice

Tuna

Crops, Industry, and Natural Resources

Salinas Bay
Cape Santa Elena

Góngora 5,670 ft/1,728 m

Santa Rosa

Papagayo Gulf

Liberia

Bagaces

Cañas

Filadelfia

Cape Velas

Santa Cruz

Nicoya

Nicoya Peninsula

Guionos Pt.

Cape Blanco

PACIFIC

GENERAL REFERENCE

Countries
COSTA RICA

San José   **Towns over 100,000**
Miramar   **Towns under 100,000**

▪▪▪▪▪ International Boundaries
〜 Major Transportation Routes
〜 Rivers

HEIGHT IN FEET AND METERS

feet	meters	
12,000	4,000	
6,000	2,000	
3,000	1,000	
1,000	300	Above Sea Level
0	0	Sea Level

0

0   5

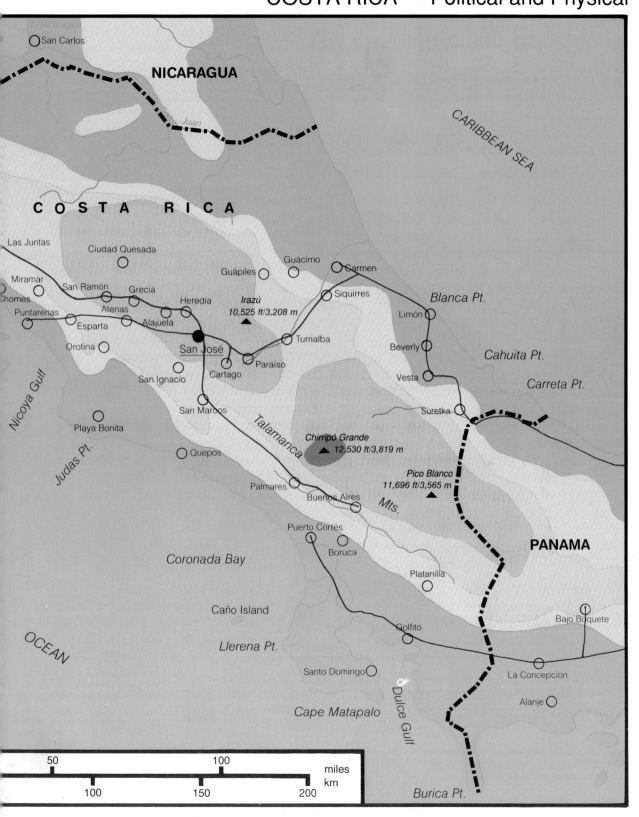

COSTA RICA — Political and Physical

NICARAGUA

San Carlos

San Juan

CARIBBEAN SEA

C O S T A   R I C A

Las Juntas

Ciudad Quesada

Miramar

San Ramón

Grecia

Guápiles

Guácimo

Carmen

Chomes

Atenas

Heredia

Irazú
10,525 ft/3,208 m ▲

Siquirres

Blanca Pt.

Puntarenas

Esparta

Alajuela

Limón

Orotina

San José

Turrialba

Beverly

Cahuita Pt.

Nicoya Gulf

San Ignacio

Cartago

Paraíso

Vesta

Carreta Pt.

San Marcos

Suretka

Playa Bonita

Talamanca

Chirripó Grande
12,530 ft/3,819 m ▲

Judas Pt.

Quepos

Pico Blanco
11,696 ft/3,565 m ▲

Palmares

Buenos Aires

Mts.

PANAMA

Puerto Cortés

Coronada Bay

Boruca

Platanilla

Caño Island

Bajo Boquete

OCEAN

Llerena Pt.

Golfito

La Concepcion

Santo Domingo

Alanje

Cape Matapalo

Dulce Gulf

Burica Pt.

50		100		miles
100	150		200	km

Land and Climate

Among the Central American countries, only El Salvador is smaller than Costa Rica. With a land area of 19,600 square miles (50,700 sq km), Costa Rica compares in size to the US state of West Virginia or the Canadian province of Nova Scotia. Located northeast of Panama and south of Nicaragua, the country has coastlines on both the Caribbean Sea and the Pacific Ocean and stretches to 175 miles (282 km) at its widest point.

Lowlands along both of Costa Rica's coasts rise to meet hills and mountains in the center of the country. The highest mountain in the country, Chirripó Grande, is about 12,500 feet (3,800 m) high. Over half of Costa Rica's people live in the *Meseta Central*, or Central Valley, which, as its name suggests, is found almost at the center of the country between ranges of mountains. Over the last two million years, the eruptions of four volcanoes have given this plateau its fertile soil. The soil combined with the area's temperate climate make the plateau perfect for farming. Several volcanoes in the highlands are still active.

The climate in Costa Rica varies from one area to another, depending primarily on altitude. In the central highlands, the climate consists of warm days and cooler nights. The average temperature in the Central Valley is 72°F (22°C). At the higher elevations, the temperature is somewhat cooler. On the coasts and in the lowlands, the climate is more tropical, with an average yearly temperature of 81°F (27°C). The hottest months are March and April. The rainy season in Costa Rica generally extends from May through November. The Caribbean coast, however, has rainfall approximately 300 days per year. Swamps and tropical rain forest cover this entire area. The Pacific coast is somewhat drier, with patches of grassland among its deciduous forests.

Natural Resources, Agriculture, and Industry

Costa Rica's most important resources are its naturally fertile soil, ample rainfall, and warm to mild climate. These factors give the country an ideal environment for growing coffee and other major crops. Other important resources include timber, seafood, and mineral deposits such as bauxite, gold, and petroleum. The country also has the conditions for producing geothermal power (energy produced through Earth's heat) and hydroelectric power (electricity generated by waterpower). Costa Rica's dams provide enough hydroelectric power to make the country self-sufficient in electricity.

Because Costa Rica has fertile soil, the nation's economy is based mainly upon agriculture. From its present production, Costa Rica feeds itself and, through improved processes, it has more surplus food to export every year. Agriculture accounts for over one-third of Costa Rica's work force. Many of these people run small family farms, growing crops such as corn, beans, and potatoes to consume and sell. Small farms also produce crops such as coffee, beef, bananas, sugar, and cocoa, but these are grown mainly for export. Increasingly, however, the larger farms control the production of these crops. In the coffee and banana industries, for example, a few large farms produce over half of Costa Rica's entire crop. Concerned about the country's dependence on a few major crops, the government encourages other crops and other industries. This way, if the demand for a crop falls, the economy can remain strong.

Manufacturing is growing quickly. It now ranks second to agriculture. Because of the country's agricultural background, food processing has become the primary manufacturing industry, followed by textiles, chemicals, plastics, clothing, fertilizer, and construction materials. Recently, tourism has also become a bigger part of the economy as more and more foreigners travel to Costa Rica to visit the country's beaches, rain forests, and national parks.

With the majority of Costa Rica's population living in the Central Valley, the valley is also the area of greatest economic activity. Private business produces most goods, although the government runs the liquor, insurance, and banking industries. The country's exports are purchased mainly by North America (35%), Western Europe (27%), and other Latin American countries (35%). Costa Rica is currently experiencing economic troubles, including a high national debt. Basically, the problem is that the country's exports are dropping in price, while its imports are rising in price.

Language

Spanish is Costa Rica's principal language. Many people — especially in the cities — also speak English, which is widely taught in the schools as a second language. Some of the black population speaks Jamaican English as its native language. The Indian languages have almost disappeared.

Education

Costa Rica's citizens are among the most highly educated people in Latin America. Over 90% of the population can read and write, probably because Costa Rica's government devotes a higher percentage of its budget to education than does any other Latin American country. Taxes provide for public school education, and the schools, in comparison to those in many developing countries, are well equipped and well funded. By law, children aged 7 to 14 must attend classes. A little over 90% of the children go on to receive at least some high school education.

Costa Rica has four national universities with a total enrollment of approximately 50,000 students. Taxes only partially support these schools. Entrance is based upon exams and academic performance, and scholarships allow many lower-income students to attend. The University of Costa Rica in San José is the largest institution of higher learning in the country. Founded in 1843, it occupies a large, modern campus. It includes schools of science, engineering, law, medicine, and liberal arts, and houses the Conservatory of Music and the Academy of Fine Arts.

Religion

Approximately 90% of Costa Rica's people are Roman Catholics. Roman Catholicism was brought over by the Spanish conquistadores and maintained by the colonists as a state religion. Under the 1949 constitution, Catholicism is still recognized as the state religion and the government is required to contribute money to help support the church. The remaining 10% of the population is made up primarily of Protestants and Jews.

Art and Culture

As is true in many of the Central American countries, Costa Rica's culture shows a mix of many ethnic groups. Predominantly Hispanic (Spanish), the country has also been influenced by its native Indian culture and the culture of North America, among others. In recent times, Costa Ricans have worked to create their own forms of art, music, clothing, and customs, incorporating traditional Hispanic and modern North American-European styles.

Costa Rica's art is a good example of this mix. The native Indians, for example, created beautiful sculptures, ceramics, and carvings of jade, gold, and stone. Many of their works have been preserved as part of a collection in the National Museum in San José, where present-day artists study this Indian art and include ideas from it in their works. Costa Rica's ethnic mix also shows in its music. Folk music throughout most of the country has a distinct Spanish sound. The use of traditional musical instruments, such as the guitar, the mandolin, the accordion, and the marimba (a type of xylophone) gives the music this character. However, on the Caribbean coast, especially near the port city of Limón, the music and dance reflect the African and Caribbean heritage of the people. Many people here favor reggae music, which comes from Jamaica and is sung in English.

Another typical display of Costa Rican folk art is the painting of carts. The heavy carts, pulled by oxen, are painted with bright-colored, detailed designs from the wheels to the yokes. No one knows the origin of this unique art form, but Costa Ricans have practiced it through many generations. When these carts were the main mode of transportation, people took great pride in decorating them.

Artists strove to create ever more intricate designs, and no two were ever alike. Eventually ox-cart painting became highly competitive. Some farmers still use these carts, especially in the more rural areas. But as cars, trucks, and other forms of transportation have replaced the carts, artists have used the well-known designs to decorate craft items.

Sports and Recreation

The most popular sport in Costa Rica is soccer. Teams form at all levels, and every vacant lot is a prime spot for enthusiastic players. The central focus of the country's love for soccer, however, is its national team. Costa Rica's national soccer team plays in matches that draw tens of thousands of spectators and are watched by thousands more on national television. When the Costa Rican national team wins an especially tough game, the streets of the capital often erupt in large, colorful celebrations.

Baseball, basketball, tennis, and track and field are other popular sports, but Costa Ricans also spend time in activities such as fishing, swimming, hiking, and camping. The country's national parks are perfect for backpacking and camping.

Costa Rica has 11 traditional holidays, some of which are religious. Many of the religious holidays are full of celebration, so Costa Ricans often take their vacations at these times. Christmas and Easter are especially big holidays, with the Easter season being the most popular time for travel. Bullfighting, parades, floats, and fireworks displays are part of these grand celebrations, in which both Costa Ricans and tourists take part.

Currency

The unit of money in Costa Rica is called the *colón*, named after Cristóbal Colón (Christopher Columbus). The colón is subdivided into 100 *céntimos*, or cents. Bills are currently printed in denominations of 50, 100, 500, and 1,000 colones. Bills of 5,000 and 10,000 colones are planned. At 1989 exchange rates, 80 colones are worth approximately one US dollar.

Costa Rican coins and paper money.

San José

Down the mountain from Sacramento lies San José, Costa Rica's capital city. San José, with a population of over 800,000, has the largest urban area in the country. Approximately one-third of the country's 2.8 million inhabitants live in the broader area in and around the capital.

The city was founded in 1737, when the capital was moved from its former site at Cartago. Present-day San José has preserved many elements from its past. A number of beautiful old Spanish colonial buildings and churches still stand near the city's center. Among these are the Teatro Nacional (National Theater), which was built in 1897, and the Palacio Nacional (National Palace), where the Legislative Assembly holds its sessions.

San José is also a modern city, with high-rise hotels, restaurants, theaters, museums, banks, government buildings, and foreign embassies. All of these are surrounded by beautiful parks and tree-lined avenues, and in the center of the city is the Plaza de la Cultura — the site for crafts vendors and art expositions. Because of the country's excellent public transportation, it is possible to travel from San José to almost any part of the country in a matter of hours.

Costa Ricans in North America

Thousands of Costa Ricans visit the United States and Canada every year. The majority come for vacation, but some come for business or to study. Former Costa Rican president Oscar Arias Sánchez studied at Boston University in Massachusetts, as did several other high government officials. Arias's wife, Margarita Penón Góngora, is a graduate of Vassar College in New York State. Few Costa Ricans, however, move north permanently. The reason why, they'll tell you, is that they like living in their own small, friendly, and prosperous country.

More Books about Costa Rica

Costa Rica. Carpenter (Childrens Press)
Costa Rica in Pictures. Lerner Publications Department of Geography Staff
    (Lerner Publications)
Fodor's Central America. (McKay)

Glossary of Useful Costa Rican (Spanish) Terms

autobús (awh-toe-BOOS) ....bus
caballo (kah-BY-yoh) ....horse

café con leche (kah-FAY KON LAY-chay) coffee with milk

Chibcha (CHEEB-chah)...........................major Indian tribe living in Costa Rica at the time of the Spanish conquest

Chorotega (chore-oh-TAY-gah)...............major Indian tribe living in Costa Rica at the time of the Spanish conquest

Don (dohn) ....title used in front of a man's name as a sign of respect

Doña (DOHN-yah). ....title used in front of a woman's name as a sign of respect

ensalada (en-sah-LAH-dah)...................salad

flan de coco (FLAHN DAY COH-coh) ....coconut custard

flor (floor) ....flower

leche (LAY-chay) ....milk

lluvia (YOO-vee-ah) ....rain

muchacha (moo-CHAH-chah) ....girl

muchacho (moo-CHAH-choh) ....boy

pájaro (PAH-hah-roh)...........................bird

parque (PAR-kay) ....park

policía y ladrónes (poe-lee-SEE-yuh E lah-DRONE-ays) ...the game of cops and robbers

tortilla (tor-TEE-yah) ....a flat, round cake usually made of cornmeal or wheat

Things to Do — Research Projects

Although it is a small country, Costa Rica has taken giant steps toward creating a peaceful, democratic society. Surrounded by nations experiencing wars and revolutions, Costa Rica has distinguished itself by becoming one of the few countries without an army. In addition, Costa Rica has succeeded in establishing and maintaining a democratic government complete with free elections and voting rights guaranteed by its constitution. After reading this book, you may want to follow Costa Rica's progress. Some of the research projects that follow need accurate, up-to-date information. Two publications that your library may have will tell you about recent newspaper and magazine articles on many topics:

Readers' Guide to Periodical Literature
Children's Magazine Guide

To find up-to-date information on topics such as Costa Rica's political situation, look up *Costa Rica* in these two publications.

1. Investigate Costa Rica as a nation without an army. What are some of the positive and negative aspects of this situation?

2. In the 1850s, US citizen William Walker invaded several Central American countries. Among other reasons, Walker wanted to add Central American nations to the United States as slave states, hoping to add strength to the US slavery movement. Imagine how Walker might have affected the Americas had he been successful in his invasion.

3. Former Costa Rican president Oscar Arias won the 1987 Nobel Peace Prize for his efforts to bring peace and stability to Central America. What kind of work did he do to earn this honor?

More Things to Do — Activities

These projects are designed to encourage you to think more about Costa Rica. They offer ideas for interesting group or individual projects for school or home.

1. Costa Rica's mountains separate the country into three different regions: the low plains, the Central Valley, and the highlands. About three-fourths of Costa Rica's people live in the Central Valley. To understand this population distribution, draw a map of Costa Rica, showing the three divisions.

2. Find out more about Costa Rica's rain forests. What is actually being done to protect them? What other measures might be effective?

3. If you would like to have a Costa Rican pen pal, write to these people:

International Pen Friends
P.O. Box 290065
Brooklyn, NY 11229

Worldwide Pen Friends
P.O. Box 39097
Downey, CA 90241

Be sure to tell them what country you want your pen pal to be from. Also include your full name, age, and address.

Index